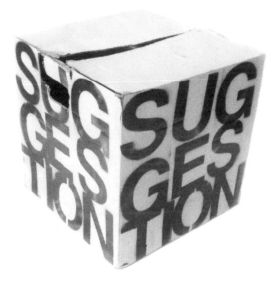

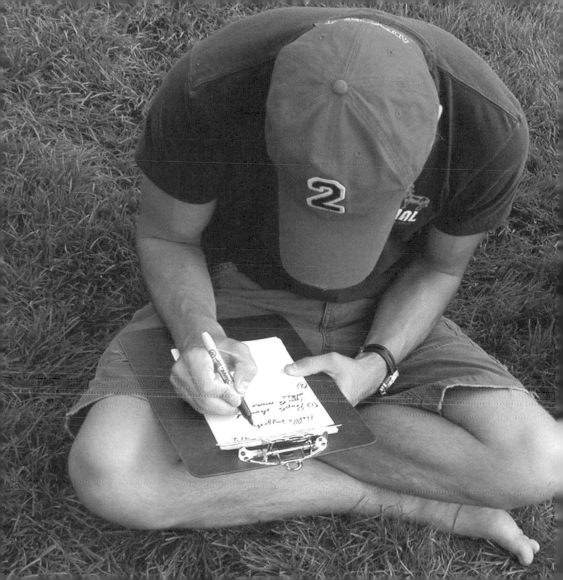

SUGGESTION

CHRONICLE BOOKS
San Francisco

Library of Congress Cataloging-in-Publication Data available.

ISBN: 0-8118-4749-7

Manufactured in China

Designed by Benjamin Shaykin
Photography by Illegal Art

Distributed in Canada by Raincoast Books
9050 Shaughnessy Street
Vancouver, British Columbia V6P 6E5

10 9 8 7 6 5 4 3 2 1

Chronicle Books LLC
85 Second Street
San Francisco, California 94105

www.chroniclebooks.com

Illegal Art is Otis Kriegel and Michael McDevitt. They both live in
New York City. Contact Illegal Art at: www.suggestionbook.com or www.illegalart.org

To the people of New York City.

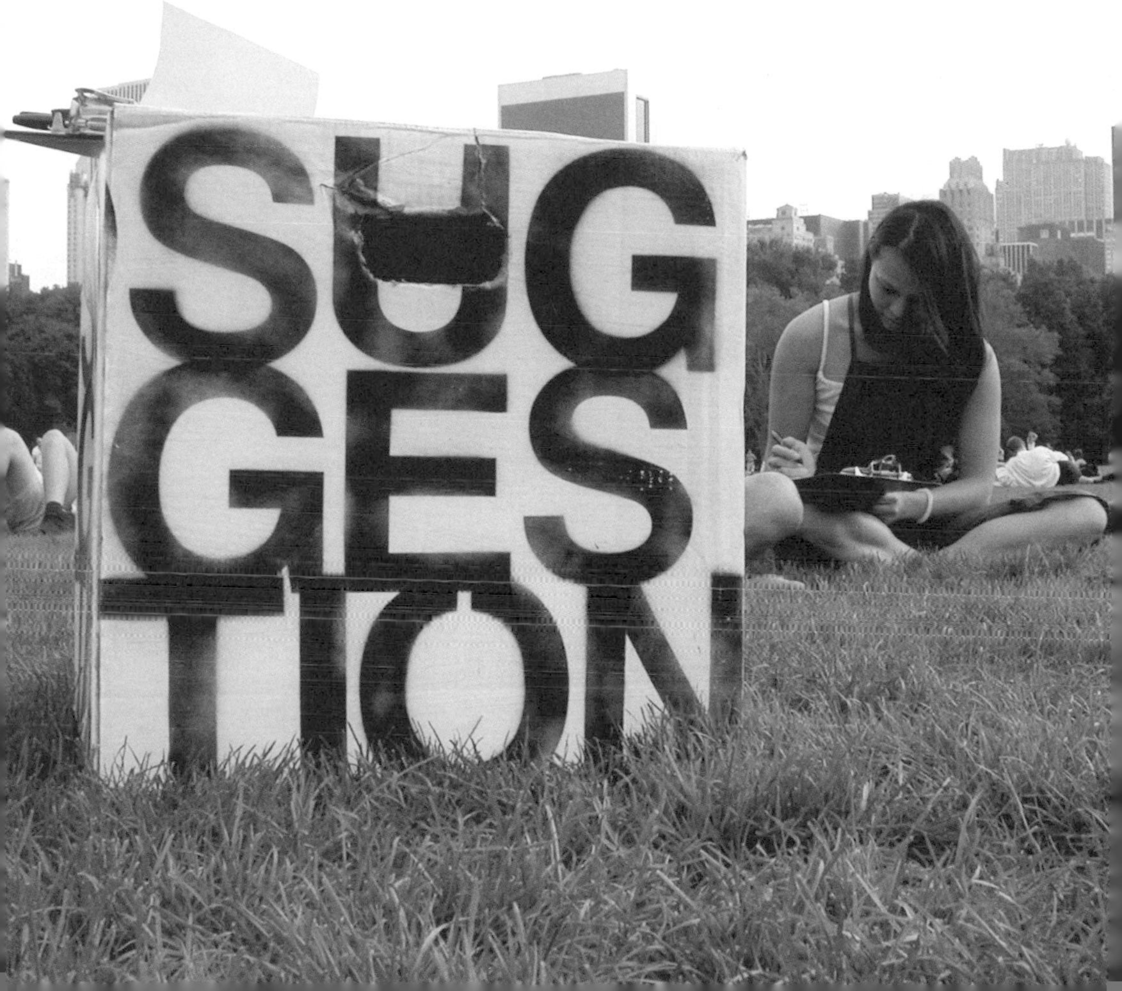
SUG
GES
TION

Contents

Introduction

"Hey, would you like to make a suggestion? About anything you want? Anything in the universe—personal, political, professional, about your friends, family? Whatever you want...."

"No! Don't tell me! Write it down. Write it down and put it in the box."

And from this simple question—armed with our white suggestion box—we collected hundreds of suggestions from all corners of New York City, from the Brooklyn Bridge to Central Park, from JFK to Grand Central, from the Lower East Side to Wall Street, from Flatbush Avenue to Lenox Avenue. Some people wrote a lot and some wrote one word. Some made far-reaching, world-changing suggestions while others voiced immediate concerns or trivial musings.

The suggestions work as a barometer of what's going on in the public's head—a quick, internal snapshot of the passerby, the person sitting next to you or across from you on the subway. Open the book and you'll read the participants' thoughts and ideas, feelings and desires, what they love and what they hate, what they want and what they want to say.

Though each suggestion is reproduced as it was originally written, there is a story behind every one. Consider the woman we followed down bustling Wall Street while she scribbled: "More time in the day." Or the man on the A train to JFK who when asked if he would like to make a suggestion said, "World peace." Or, at the base of the Brooklyn Bridge, a

woman who sadly wrote her suggestion and then held it up for us to read: "Don't ever brake [sic] up with someone on a bridge." Another woman wrote: "My friend, Jonathan, should kiss me," as she stood next to, of all people, Jonathan. Some people chased us down and held us prisoner while they wrote suggestion after suggestion. Others did their best to avoid us, but then came scrambling back with a sudden idea.

Of the more than 1,800 suggestions that we've collected over the past three years, not all could be included. It was a challenge to find a balance between themes and originality, such as the popular "legalize marijuana" versus the rare soul who told us pointedly to "mind the gap." We labored to balance the voice of the crowd with the voice of the individual.

These suggestions might shock you, inspire you, crack you up, or break your heart. But as you turn the pages, consider it a way to connect with others, a glimpse into what everyday people are thinking, feeling, and seeing in our world. You might not be the only one who has that idea, and you might be surprised by the originality of others.

And most of all, if you see us walking down the street with The Box, please, make a suggestion.

—Illegal Art

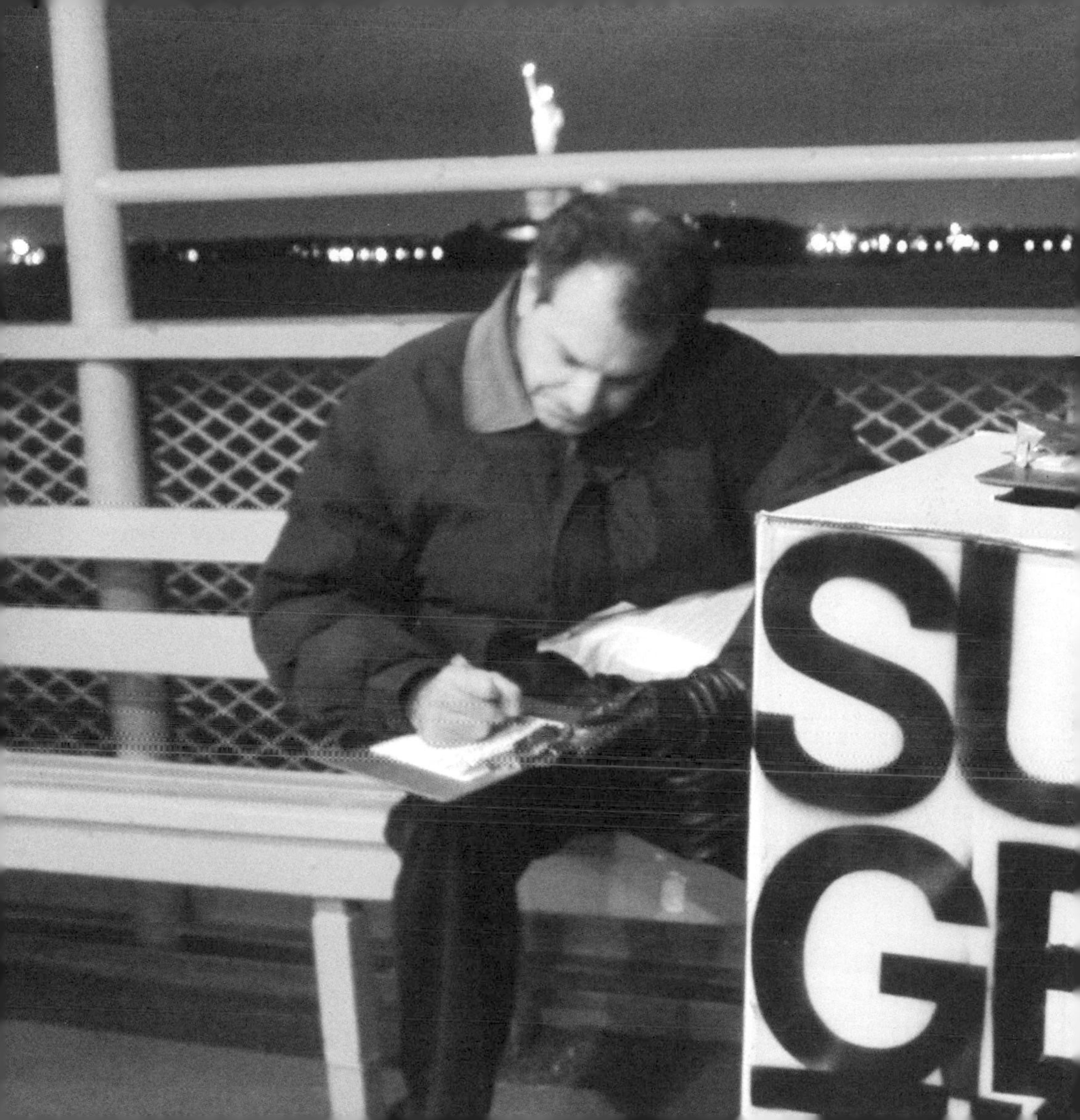
SU
GE

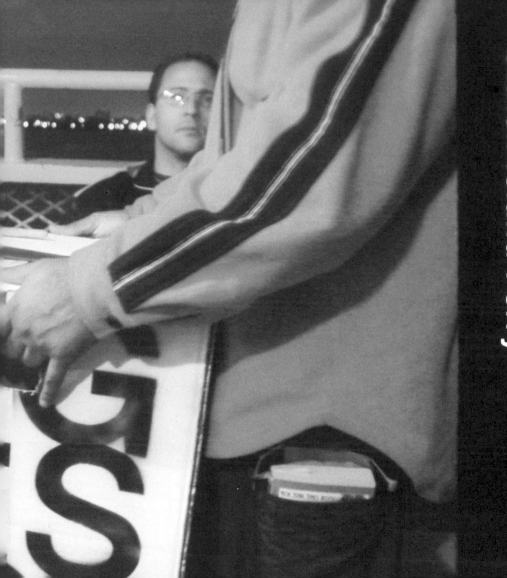

Staten Island Ferry

Make The

S. I. Ferry

Run Every

15 minutes

24 hrs.

Free
pumpkin pie

every

thursday.

I SUGGEST
AMERICA TO
BRUSH UP ON
HER MANNERS.
HAVE RESPECT
AND PATIENCE
FOR ELDERLY,
~~WOMEN WITH CHILDREN~~
AND PREGNANT
WOMEN.

Remember What Your Cause
And Purpose is

RMS

Why do we have
to do meaningless
shit just to pay
bills?

cheaper
yu-gioh cards.

Bunny

ears

for

everyone

I suggest everyone accept Jesus Christ as their Lord and Savior.

THE OPPORTUNITY
TO GET A JOB

I think we SHOULD BE ABLE to DRINK iN public.

Always wipe front to Back

MORE $$

FOR EMT'S

Why is it okay for us to go to war but we still can't leagly drink

<u>Beer</u>

Honda's Look
likE lAmoqinis

Me gustaría que la gente visitara más este país, porque yo he venido de vacaciones con miedo, pero ~~cada vez que~~ cuanto más lo conozco, más me gusta.

♡

MORE
Free
day care
for teenage
Parents.

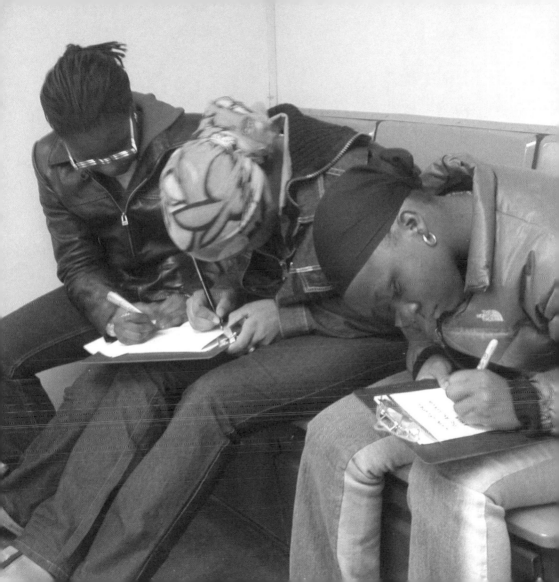

Better to let people think
you're stupid than open
your mouth and prove it.

Love
EACH OTER
- OR -
Perish.
- Morrie!

① never purchase ō
insurance.

② never purchase
a physician

③ purchase
a nurse !

④ never own a
car

⑤ never tow a
trailer ⟶

⑥ own a hitch

⑦ a master card

⑧ own a visa
— it's express.

33

Make
it
easier

MAINTAIN RESTROOMS
IN S.I. FERRY TERMINAL
TO AN ACCEPTABLE
STANDARD- ASK THE
SPOUSE OF THE DIRECTOR
OF FERRY SYSTEM IF
HE/SHE WOULD FEEL
COMFORTABLE USING THEM

Protest Tomorrow

e

DO A FAVOR
FOR
SOME ONE

The ~~Food~~ on this ~~Boat~~
Sucks!!

Pay me and fellow
members of the
NYPD's finest
get paid better.

LNF

OUT CALL

ORGANIZED

RECIGEON

Please Legalize

Marijuana!!!

A merry-go-round
in my backyard

My husband make more money.

My Kid cries less.

My mother wasn't so ~~opini~~ opinionated.

some skates
for my ~~brithday~~
brithday

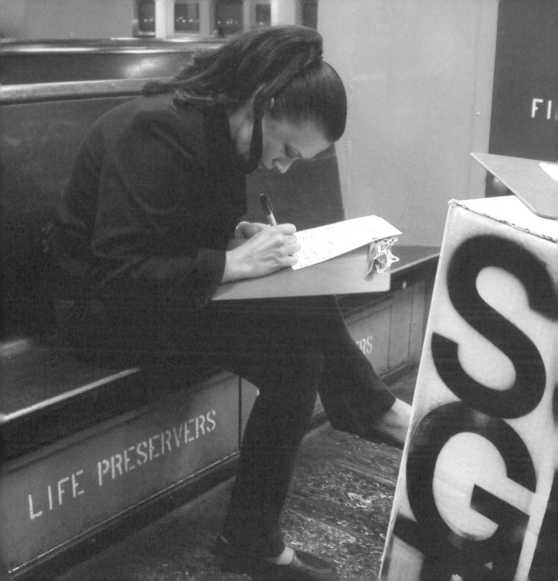

I Think
Clinton Should
Be president
Again
and Drugs
Should Stay
Illegal

My, sugestion IS . . .

FOR COPS TO STOP

MESSIN WITH ME

BECAUSE I'M STANDING
WITH FRIENDS thinkin
I'M GONNA SHOOT
MY FRIEND...
[PREVIOUS ACCIDENT]

SCRAP DADDY.
e.N.4 - STATEN

Americans need to think globally. We consume too much and only think of ourselves! I suggest we cover this IN the media!

Quisiera la paz para
todo el mundo

The mayor should better the city by Having Less crime, because safety is the the first THING for all of us.

I suggest
you give
me the
box.
— Katie &
Anne 17
Staten Island.

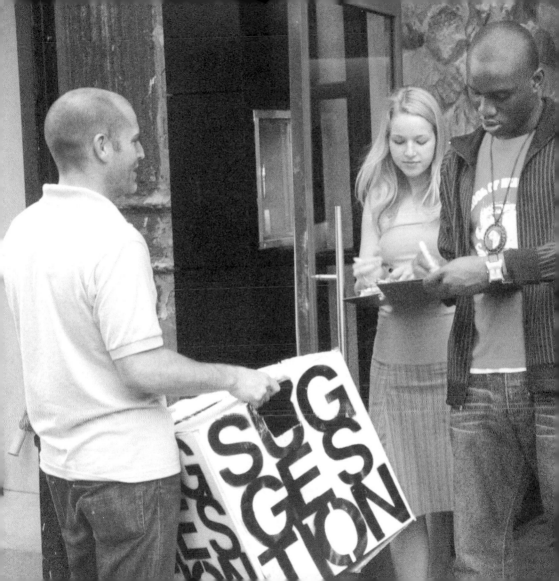

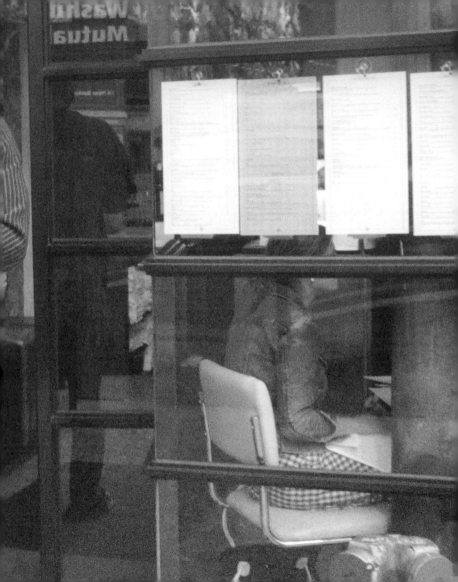

1. WEAR SILK BOXERS

2. KILL THE SLUMLORDS

3. HUMOR IS UNDER-RATED

Wonder Bras
are over rated.

NEVER GET A

~~ROOMATE~~ ROOMMATE

instead of working æ to develop a pill for erectile disfunction, scientists should develop a " good manners" pill.

I suggest all white guys
w/ dreads cut their
hair and donate ~~it~~ it
to stuffed animal
factories

THINK TWICE
BEFORE ACTING...

Women should be perceived as sexy in flat shoes, in a perfect world

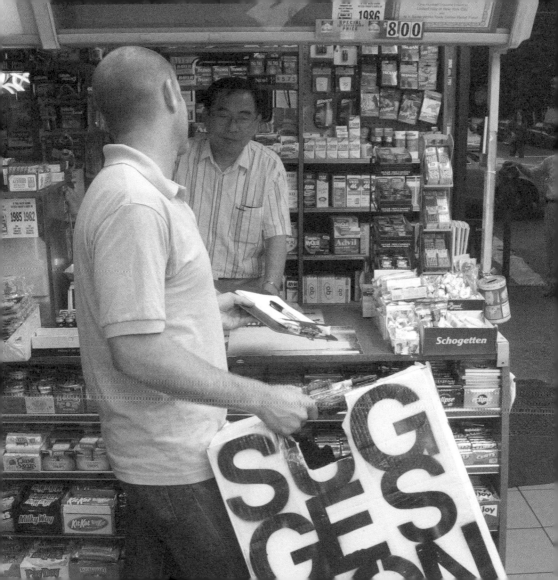

Outlaw public art projects so that I won't get bothered in the street.

Less Duane Reade's
everywhere —
more consumer
friendly establishments.

Duck-
Tape
your
Roommate !
~~and~~ When leaving

Bruce

visit thy
bronx zoo

Put comfortable seats in woman clothing stores in order .to make ~~the~~ shopping experience ~~could~~ more pleasent for men who "tag"/ we forced along.

All
Apt.
Should be
$200 ...

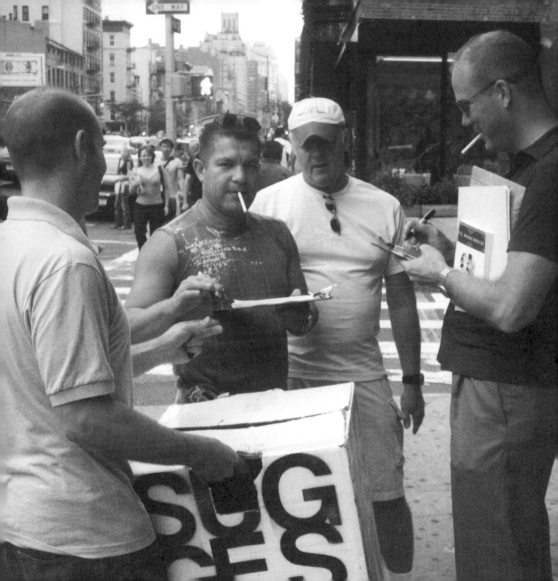

I suggest that more people RELAX.

It's really no big deal.

Promise.

No more gender specific language when greeting a stranger.

Ginko trees should be planted everywhere.

I suggest the greenpeace
people try wearing red.

Remote control devices
should be <u>white</u> with black
letters (rather than the reverse)
Who can read those black
remote controls in the dark?

Please, all women,
enjoy   dessert.

I wish my boyfriend would pay my bills.

So I wouldn't have to keep working these bullshit job !!!

GAY MARRIGE
A

IN NY!

Don't let the
Super run the
whole street!

give
me
a
Break.

IRMA

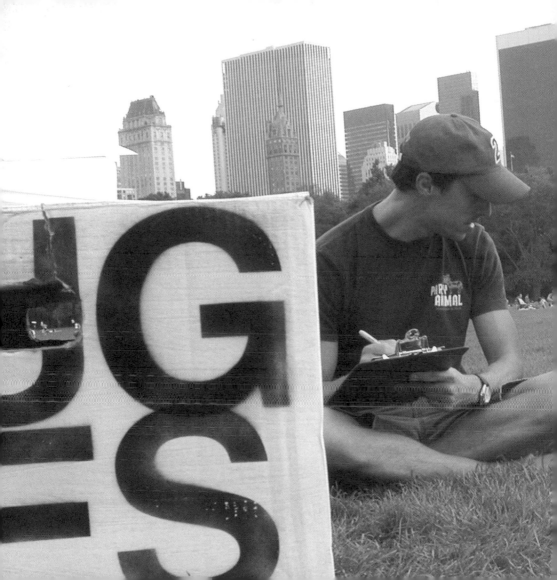

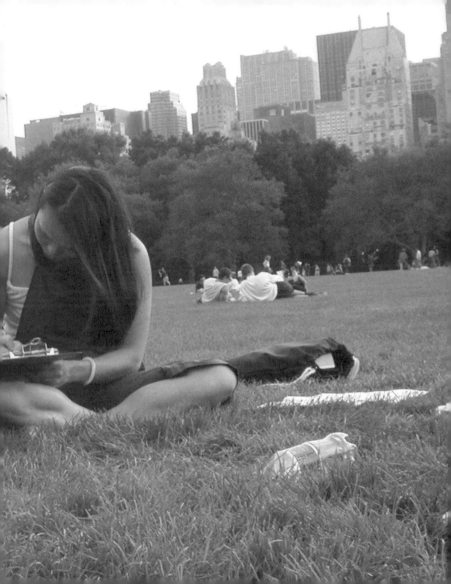

I suggest that
every weekend should
be a three day weekend.

Always spank
your Kids.

ALWAYS USE

condoms

Always keep a bucket
of bleach on hand.

The government should supply tampons free of charge to women.

Keep your mouth
shut sometimes.

שתויים   יוכלו   לקבל

ארין   כותב   הללגנו

ALWAYS KNOW WHO
YOU INVITE TO YOUR
Home. . . .

you should have
snacks

That the world be
covered in linoleum
so we could tap
dance all day!

-Adam

KEEP IT

SIMPLE

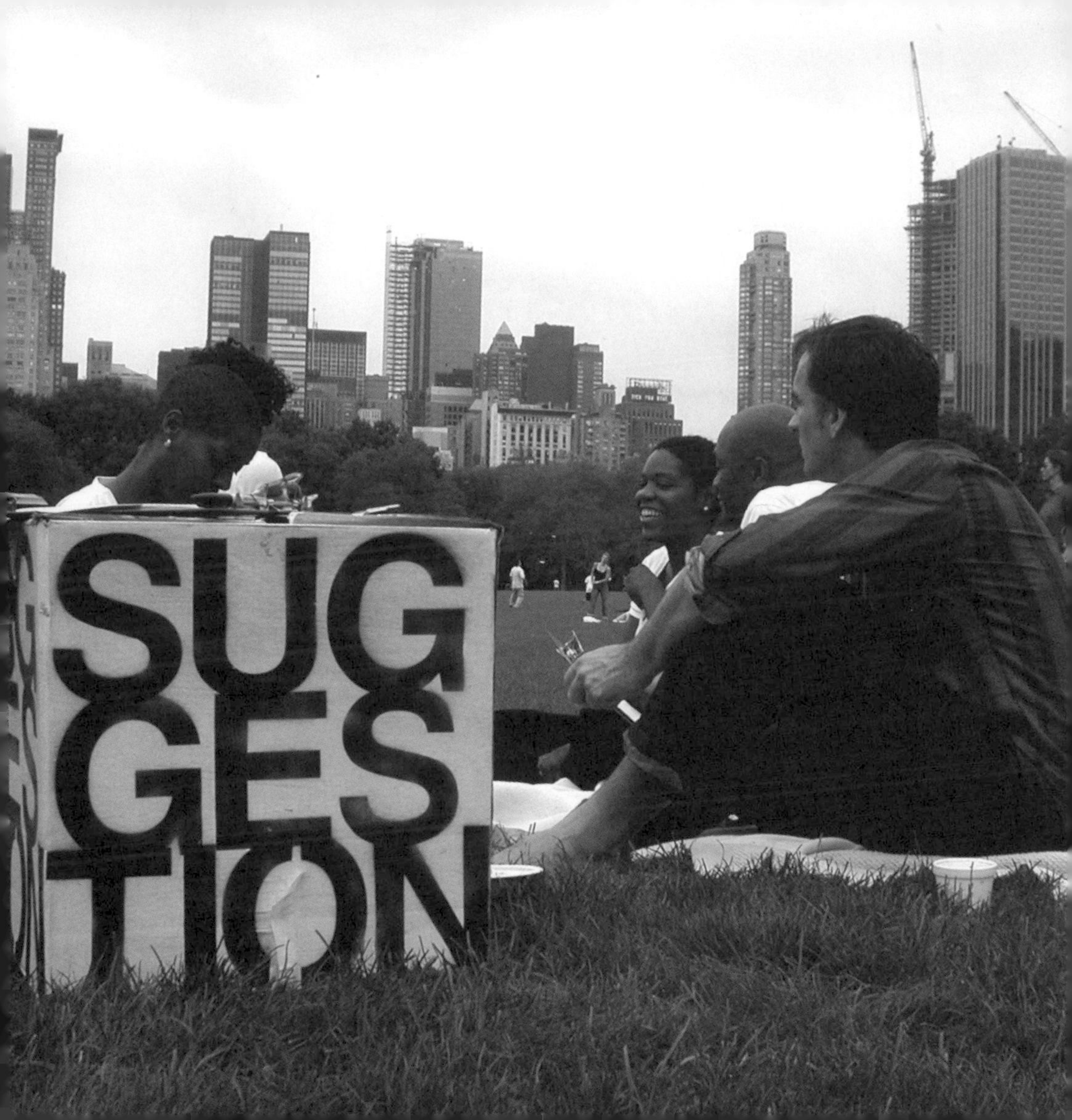
SUG
GES
TION

FOR GALS: think
if audrey
hepburn would
do whatever your
Contemplating. If
she would than
you probably
should too.

I SUG-GEST THE CHICKEN

fill all the
subway
tunnels
with art that
animates as the
train moves.
(like on the D train)

Give Xiaoying some new shoes.

Take your shirt off

take breath
Mints when
offered

I suggest that they
stop suggestion boxes

MORE

BOLLYWOOD

Don't have children until you are ready to!

1. Take everyone in Israel + move them to France Then move everyone from France to Israel.

2. No Smoking in the Meadow.

3. No Brits in the Meadow.

4. Coffee/sandwich Bar in Meadow.

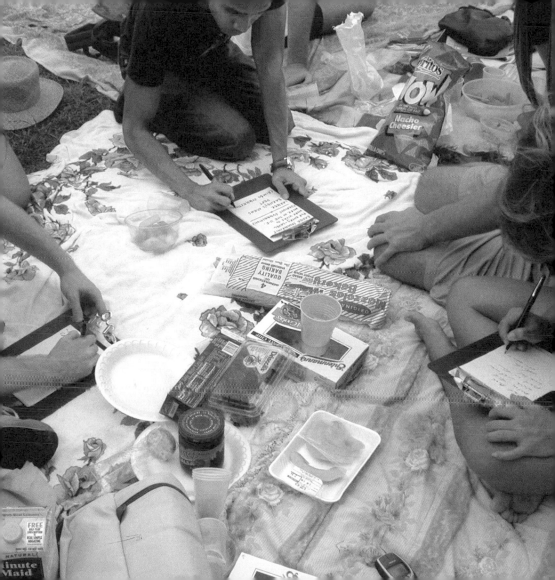

I suggest you avoid the Van Wyck.

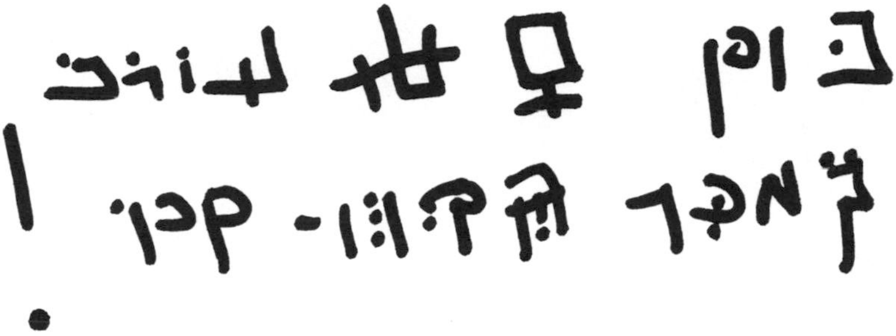

I think that when Burger King says that they have a 99¢ menu in the New York, it should be 99¢, not $1.49 becuse

I have an extra dollar and not $1.50 so it fucks every thing up and you can afend 7¢ every where or ask some one for it

i SUGGEST
YOU
mIND
THE
GAP

Never Talk
Shit to the
Person who's
house your
Visiting.

its all right

I suggest that society accept polygamy as the natural state.

EASIER SPONSORSHIP
FOR ENTRY - LEVEL
WORK VISAS TO
WORK IN THE U.S.
(SERIOUS SUGGESTION)

LARGER
BARNEy's MENS
DEPT

(BIMBO SUGGESTION)

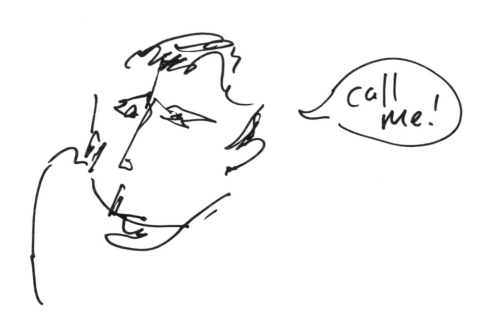

American people
should be
less
individualistic
======

(be more human)
2 french tourists

All of NY to contribute
$1 to the "Heather & Kris
fund for underprivileged
newly weds"!!

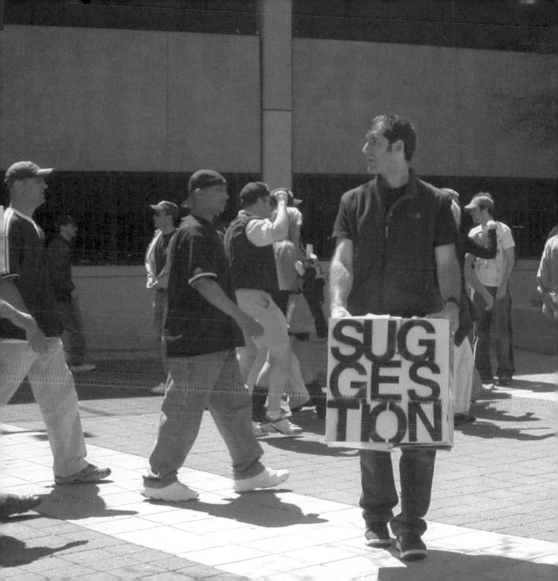

4 Train to Yankee Stadium

I Better not lose my money on the YANKS today.

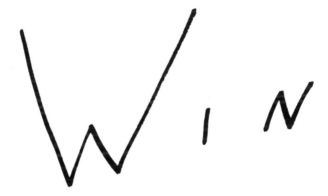

Let's
Make a
better
world

We should get free
T-shirts.

Better
pitching

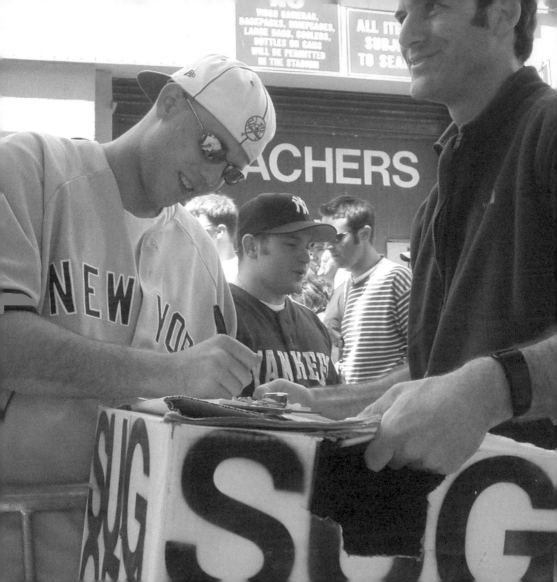

GO

RED SOX !

A · ROD

.000

FREE
TICKETS
FOR KIDS

I suggest
that the Red Sox
quit playing baseball.

National Bikini
Arts Day.
Think of the fans!

GET

MORE

SLEEP

Be there early.

Don't be
late!

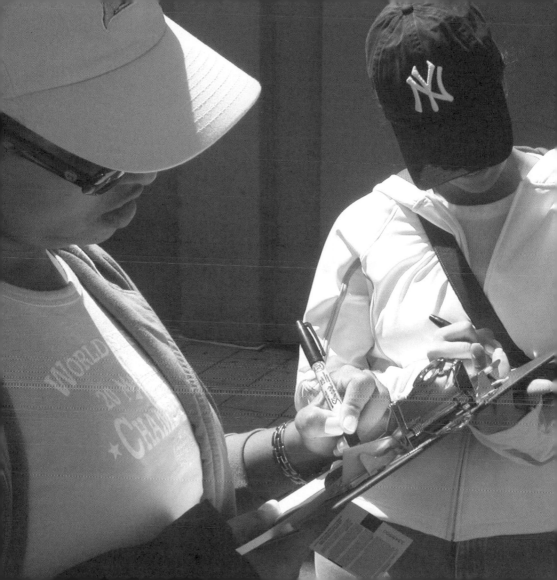

I should of
had Breakfast.

Wisdom teeth
aqht to evolve
sooner or later.

I what the

YanKEE to win

Free

Beer

More free beer.

I SUGGEST that
PEOPLE ~~will~~ should
STOP DRINKING
AND FIND OTHER WAYS
TO SOLVE THEIR
PROBLEMS.
AND BE MORE REALISTIC
ABOUT THE WORLD
SURROUNDING THEM

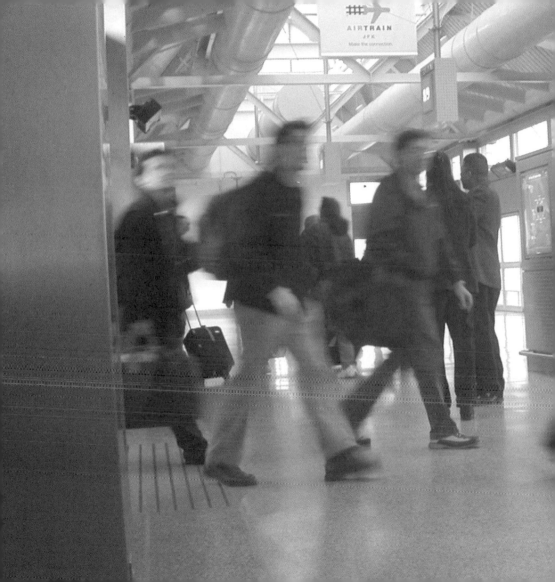

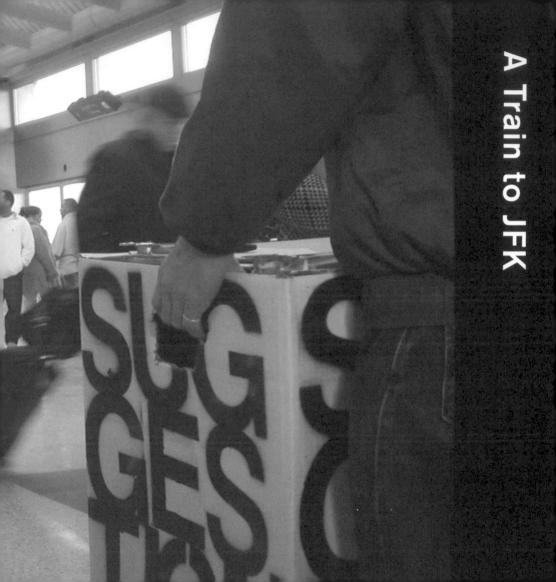

A Train to JFK

Stop treating
Canadian
immigrants
like
Mexicans!

① MAKE TAX FORMS SIMPLER

② LET POLITICAN FILL OUT A 1040 TAX FORM TO SEE HOW EASY IT IS

THey Need the 11 foot
riM.

MORE BLACK People in the U.S. Government

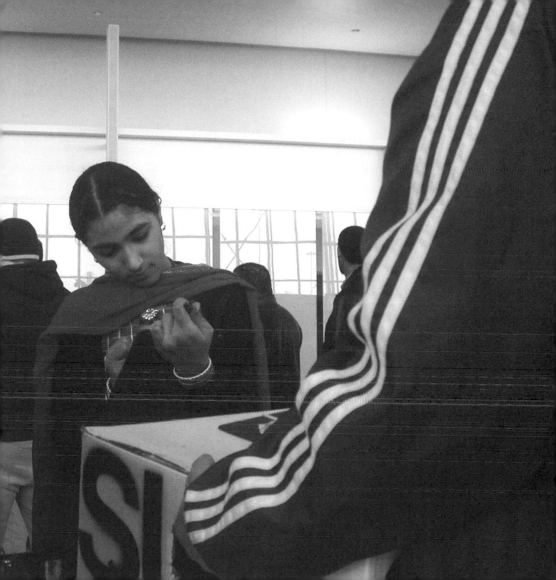

I think JFK airport should have more seats offered to people that are waiting for arrivals of their relatives.

People should
be more willing
to have
monkeys as
Pets.

Find Marius
from Vienna
International
School

I

want

Him to

Get a life.

Seeing as i am British
& we are renowned for bad
weather i propose that all
umbrellas should become public
property so you leave them at
the door of a building & pick
up a new one when you leave.

World peace

I suggest, instead of reparations for the enslavement of African Americans, create uplifting programs for the inner city youth. Create better and more schools and more educational programs teaching about economics.

Do the
Right thing
By your Kids.

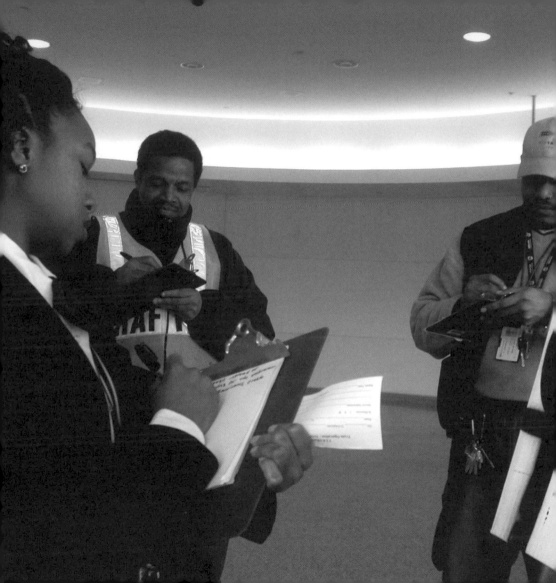

More leg room on airplane economy class, w/o watching video on wonderful features of business class . . .

Stop saying
"Hi, How ya doin"
when you don't
mean it, and you're
programmed to say
it.

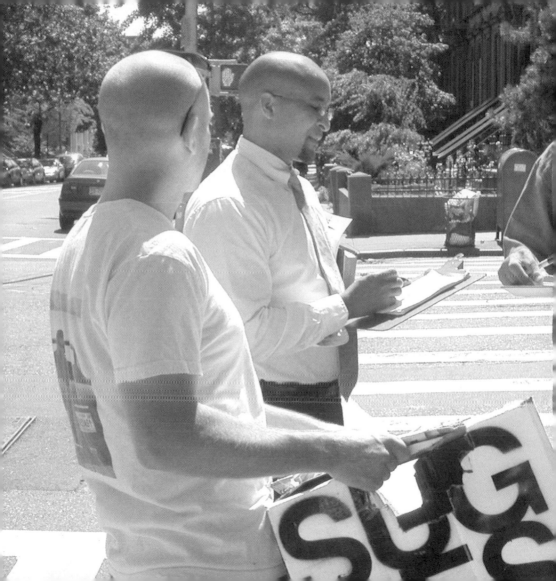

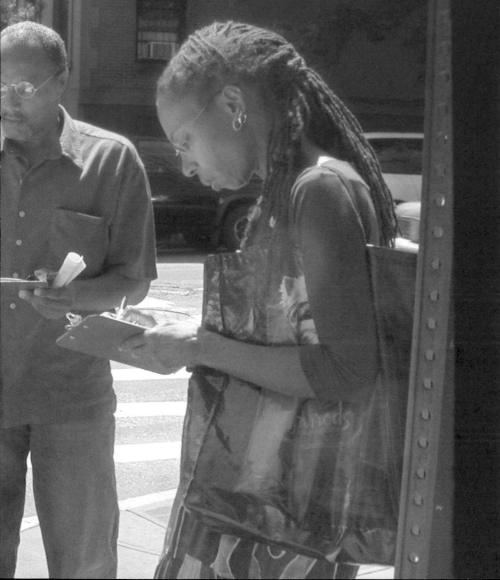

I don't think
it is fair that
housing projects
are isolated in
areas where there
is nothing (ie - no
real organization, museums
etc).
I suggest that they
be placed in richer
neighborhoods

think of human
beings in general
as a special
interest group

o bliterate

the

word

Carbohydrate

Our Greatest Weapon
against Terrorism is

Education.

JOB TO BE EASIER TO GET.

MORE MONEY FOR EDUCTION

SEX FOR ALL OVER 70

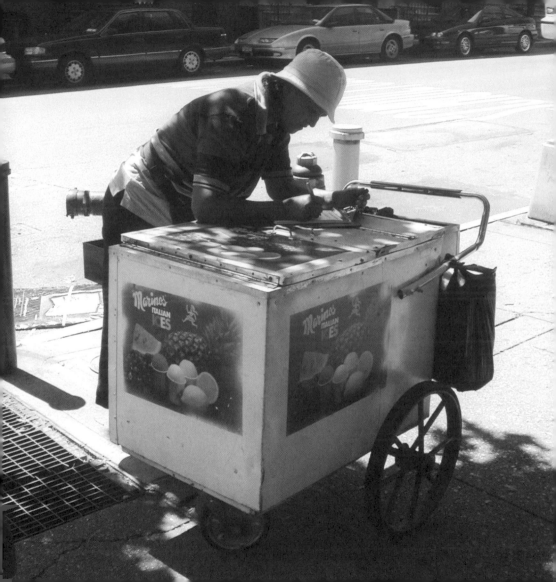

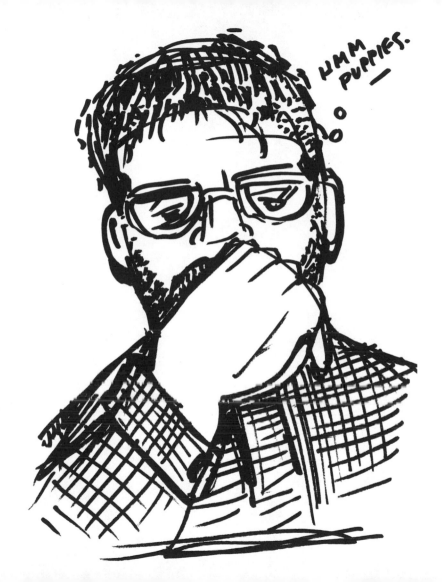

I suggest anyone
that pays the additional
.30 ¢ to dial the phone
after calling information
seriously reevaluate
their life.

I think we should
GET RID OF
ALL THE TREES
AND PUT GIGANTIC
tootsie ROllS INSTEAD
OF EACH ONE .

Beer flavored nipples

18 year old adults
Should have more
~~preveliges~~ priveligies.

A COURTESY FLUSH

IS ALWAYS A

MUST.

LEARN HOW TO BE A GOOD KISSER!

9/11/2022

انا احب
الحريه والعداله
وسلام
واحب الجميع
البشر

كل نفسراح المخرب

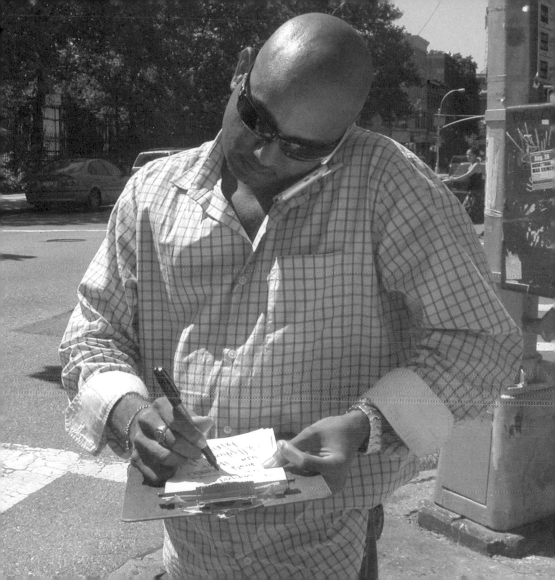

Mel should shut ter masth

capable of. You'll surprise
yourself.

(17) ~~Gauge~~ Gauge your anger.

(18) Be honest, but know when to
be gentle.

(19) Adopt an animal.

(20) Be open to falling in love.

(21) Read Douglas Adams

(22) Support your friends
passions. No matter how
far fetched.

(23) Make forts with blankets
and watch movies.

(24) Love unconditionally

(25) Forgive.

(26) Forget.

(27) See #24

Empower the doves

Declaw the hawks

God .

REGULATE THE SALE OF
TELEVISIONS TO ONLY
THOSE WHO PASS
LITERACY STANDARDS.

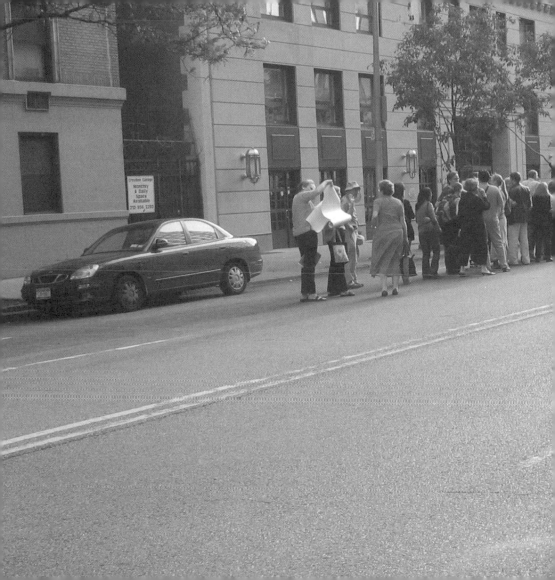

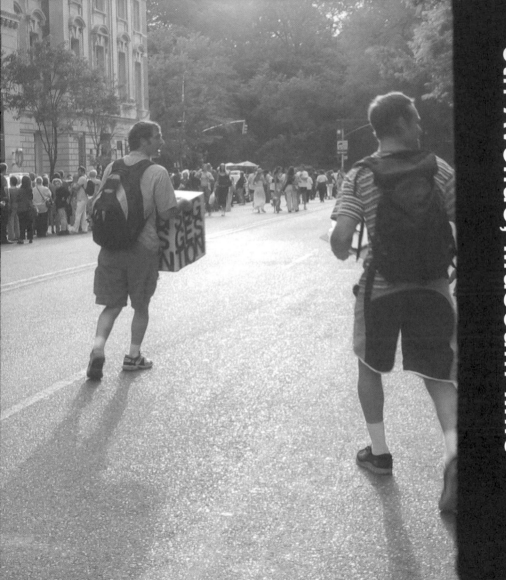

GET

A LITTLE

CLOSER

lower transit
Fear

EVERYONE IN
AMERICA SHOULD
NOT WATCH
TV FOR ONE
MONTH.

LARGER
INTANGIBLE
OBJECTS.

Two Words:

More Mullets!

I suggest I should have a date this Sat. night.

I want more
celery in my
Salad.

I suggest that there be A National Holiday named after me

DREHON

IT SHOULDN'T
BE CALLED
"BLUE".
IT SHOULD
BE CALLED
"RONK".

All hot *girls* ~~guys~~ should be bisexual.

TELL THE
TRUTH,
DAMMIT/

.

why does
the WAX in
my ear taste
so weird ??
‖
∧

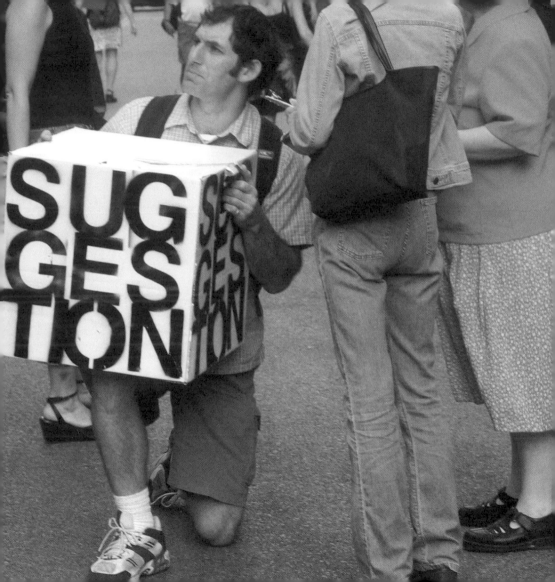

Don't put
off today
what you
may have
done yesterday.

Every college graduate in NYC should have to teach for a semester in their subject area in an inner city school (for free)
↳ underpriveledged school

Jess

We Should
all Go to

Italy

I suggest sex
for everyone at
least once a day

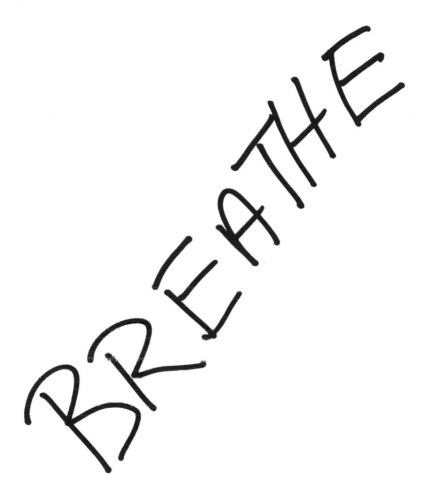

eat shit

- LET'S MAKE ~~MAKE~~ TUTUS MANDATORY

- THE FRICK SHOULD BE
  INCLUDED

- I WANT TO BE AN ~~AN~~ ALCOHOL
  MODEL

flying cars
OR
human WINGS

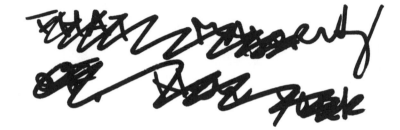

✳ Quik-naps

STORAGE FACILITIES — STREET
FRIENDLY — (SLEEPING) FOR
            FOR
EXHAUSTED, ANGRY, OVERWORKED
NEW YORKERS.

$25 FOR 25 MIN.

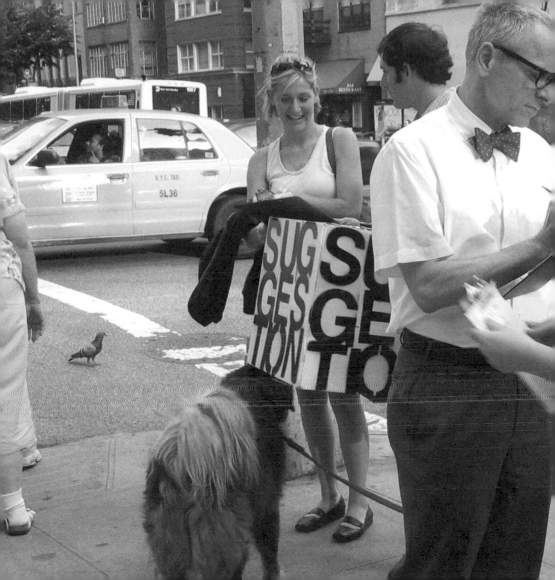

I think the
"Wait 3 days rule"
should be changed
to the "wait 2
hours rule"

Strong laws limiting
who can wear
cut off tops

Can taxi drivers stop
threatening to kill me
while driving straight at
me?

Have one day on which people from each neighborhood go into their local subway station and all work together to scrub it. If there were enough people, everyone would only be responsible for about 3 feet, and that's not overwhelming at all!

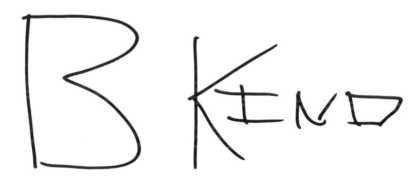

MY BOYFRIEND
SHOULD BE
ON TIME & BUY
A CELL PHONE.

I LOVE
MONEY
PUT ME
MONEY
IN MY
BANK

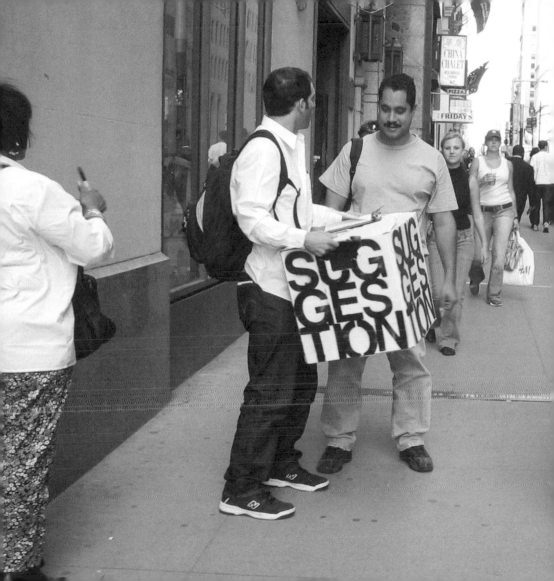

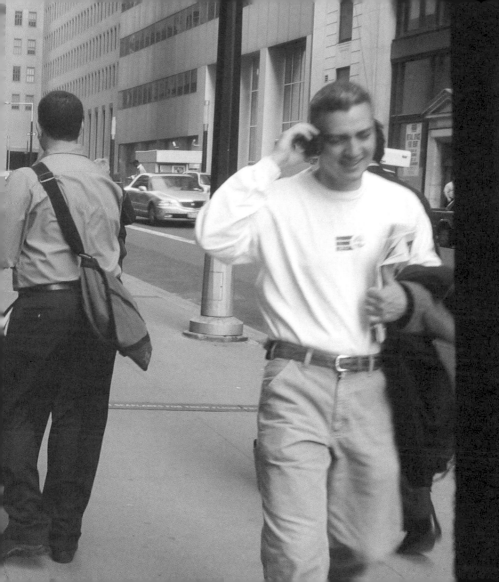

Wall Street

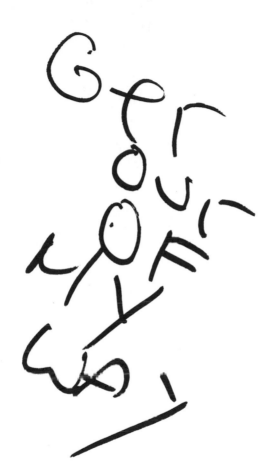

more time
in the
Day.

I suggest money being sent to my house.

Go ahead +
have that
ice-cream cone
Tonight

Don't
wear
Plaid .

———————⟶

less
ties

Changing
NYC
from the
'Big Apple'
to the
'Big Banana'

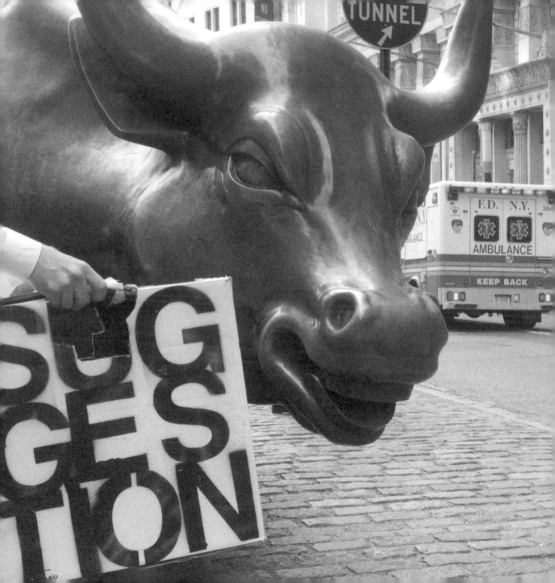

No more rounded bottoms on plastic soda bottles !

ARABS
Should
Be
Outlawed

CHEESE
FRIES !
NOW !

I suggest that
girls shouldn't
wear Panties.
"Or at least
grandma Panties".

I suggest
that the
Weed oN S.I
Should be
a higher grade.

Abolition of
Death penalty.
in The USA.

Leave no trace

Redistribute
taxes so
that the
wealthy share
a larger
fat Burden

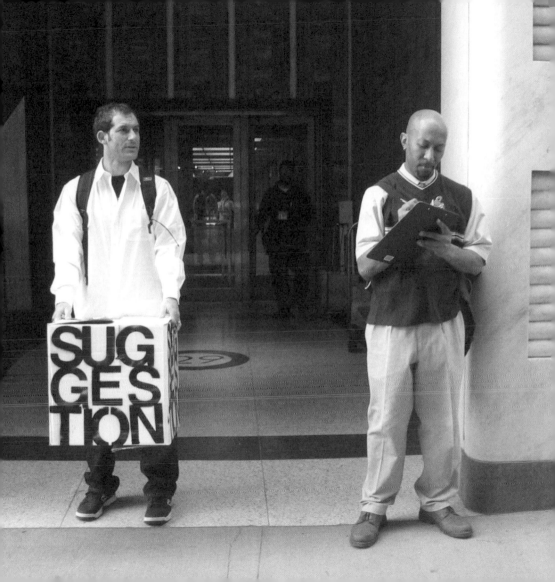

MAKE
Money instead
of
Suggestions

EVErY oNe
Should
SWiM
With
DOLPh iNS-

— Maia

I suggest that
Dave stops wasting
my precious time.

I sussest
you don'T

AskFor
SussesTions?

Because No one
Is going To
give u my
SussesTions

I hate
Fat chicks
who walk
up sch way
steps with
thongs.

Tell all Terrorist
To blow their
families to

Pieces—

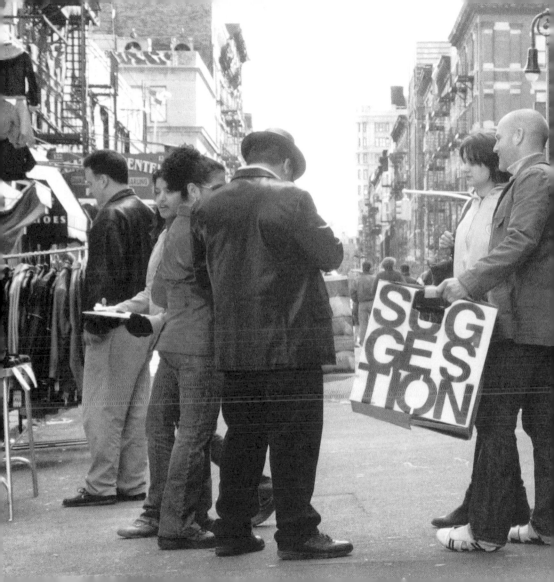

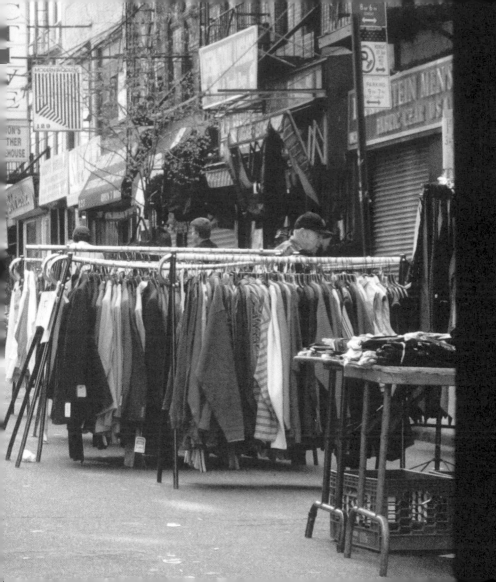

Lower East Side

BARRY NEEDS
TO GET
BETTER
TASTE

That fire engines
don't honk — we
can hear the
siren already.

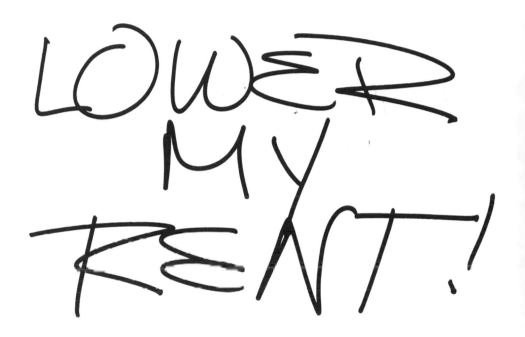

I suggest that we drive
every automobile in to
the ocean

Get
Zinnia to
quiet the
fuck
down
(we're not square)

MIKAEL NEES TO
CHANGE HIS NY
FUCKIN' ATTITUDE
& REMEMBER WHO
HE REALLY IS!

DRAG PARADE
w/ GO GO BOYS
Margaritas

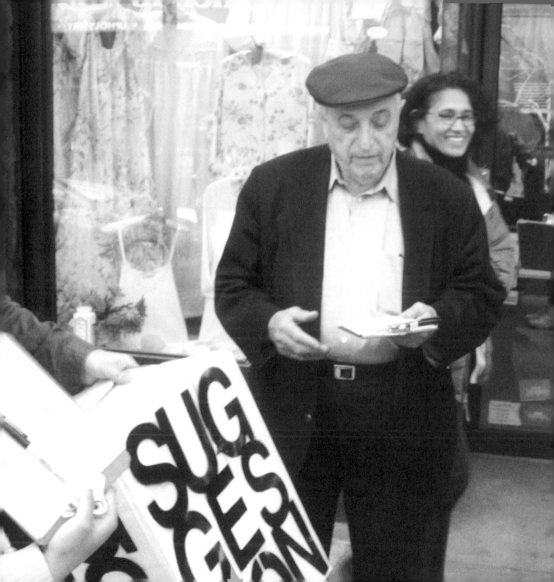

to my husband: ~~smoke~~
<u>Small</u> cigars

More
dogruns !

I suggest
that Rio
buy me
Dim SUM

NO music
when you are
on hold on
the telephone.
Silence, please!

CHOOSE WISELY !

Need to have Jewish area on map

Stop
Lying

All world leaders In one
room — The one who speaks
the shortest time wins all

Give Palestine
back
to
Palistinine

a boy who loves
polka dots. .

not 1950's ones
1890's ones

Move to
Vermont

LIVE

IN

THAILAND

The people should
police themselves

DON'T SLEEP W/ A
GIRL ,WHEN YOU &
YOUR ROOMATE HAVE
SOMETHING GOING ON &
THEN BRING HER HOME.
AND HAVE YOUR ROOMMATE
HAVE TO MEET HER IN THE
MORNING. OR DON'T GET INVOLVED W/ ROOMMATE.

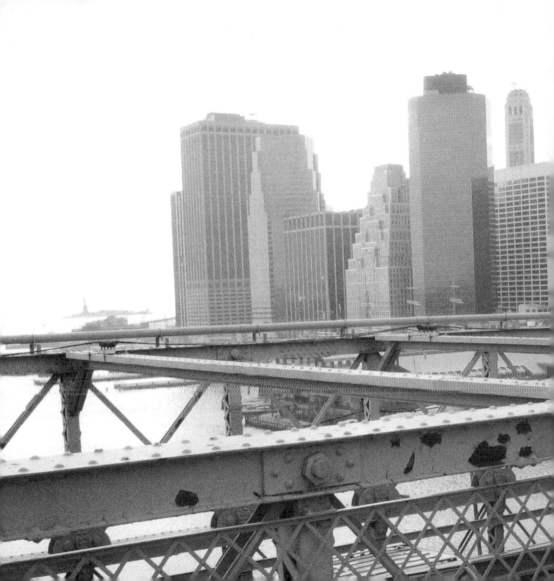

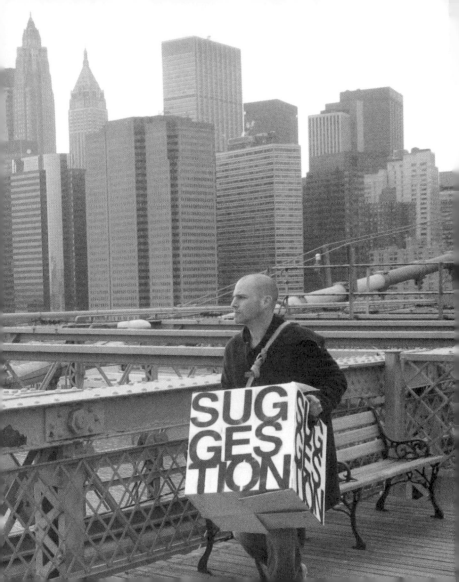

AWESOME. SCENERY & A BIG. CITY
& A DAMM. FINE. BRIDGE

WALK
EVERYWHERE.

SLOWLY.

U.S. OUT OF
ALL OVER
(EVERY WHERE)

Beer w/out Borders

CANDIDATES

THAT MAKE

ME

WANT TO

VOTE

more men in kilts

I suggest that people stop flying planes into buildings.

My friend, Jonathan, should kiss me.

UNIVERSAL HEALTH CARE

GO

FOR A

WALK WHEN

IT'S NICE OUT

CALL
YOUR MOTHER
MORE

DO
A
GOOD
JOB

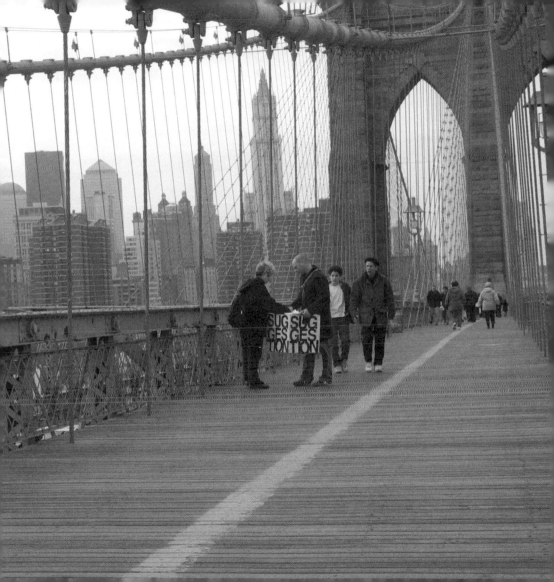

THIS BRIDGE IS BEAUTIFULL, BUT GIVE IT A LICK OF PAINT.

GET THE

U.S.A.

A DIVORCE

FROM

OIL.

NY SHOULD BECOME A SEPERATE COUNTRY

fo wax
da† ass!

STAND ON ONE LEG LIKE
A FLAMINGO.

Don't ever brake up
with someone on
a bridge

Get Rid of the
Petty ~~thieves~~ Criminals in our
Prisons and use
that space for
Real Ones!!

Free elephAnT rides
Across The bridge.

ASK MORE QUESTIONS.

Do Something About

All This.

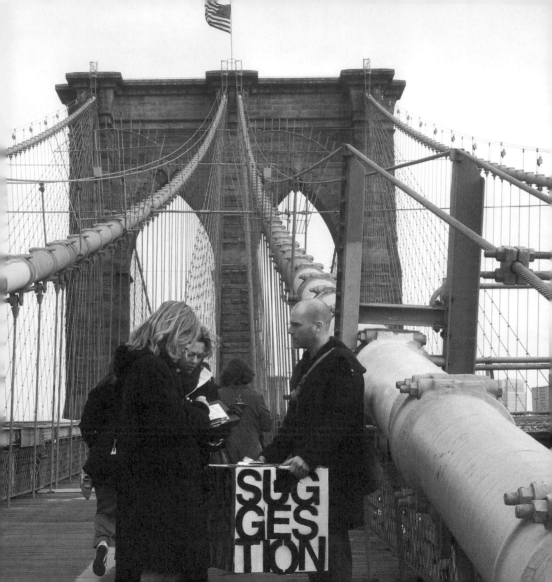

That we have more public holidays
and less Jewish ones.

TOILET SEAT WARMERS ARE
VERY COZY. CHECK IT OUT.

There should be a time everyday
when people in offices all over the
city should stop work, go outside
and scream REALLY LOUDLY.
(a moment of noise, rather
      than silence.)

很好的地方. 治安和衛生
都比想像中好

NICE CITY

再蓋兩棟 WTC 吧

Make them pay!

Do what you love
Today.

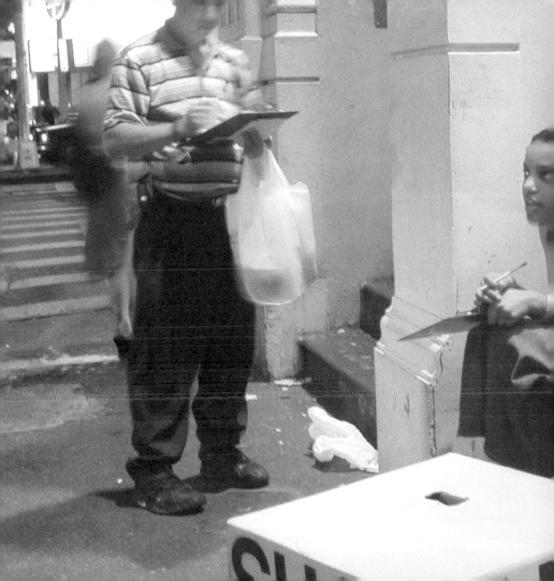

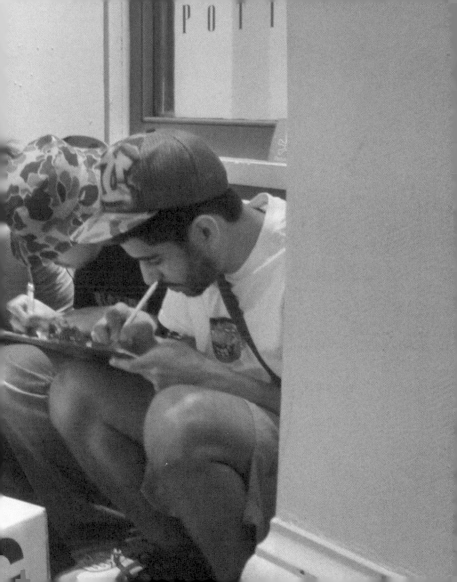

I suggest that kids have a chance to go to summer camp.

men should
love their women
better.

I'd like to suggest that the Hassidic men consider a lighter summer look.

PUT A FLOWER
IN YOUR HAIR

Why do guys bother
calling at 11:45 pm
& say they just want
to hang out when
what they really
want is just to fuck.
Just say "hey, can I come
over and fuck?"

I'M JUST KIND OF EMPTY TONIGHT

SEND ME A
MILLION DOLLARS
& LET ALL MY
JAIL NIGGAS
FREE -

HAVOC

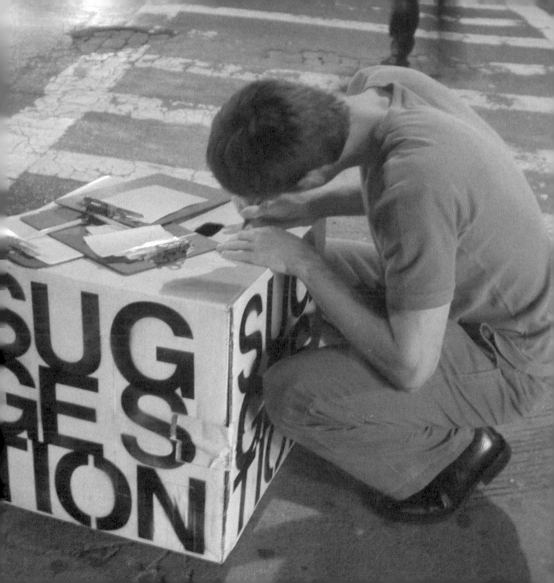

<u>Rounded Edges</u>
on all objects!!!
We have all cut,
banged, bumped etc.
ourselves unnecessarily
on sharp corners+edges.

Cushioned Pavement

CABS CANNOT GO OFF
DUTY AT 4-6 PM.

SHE SHOULD DATE ME

LIFE
Should
Be shorter

Tell the older generations to stop giving advice to the younger generation

I suggest that grocery stores be required to lump all the preservative-laden chemically foods together under a big sign reading "Toxic."

I suggest everybody eats pancakes and chicken every morning

Buy me a drink

Explore your elbows

GOVERNMENT SUBSIDIZED
DISTRIBUTION OF FREE
CHUCK TAYLORS FOR ALL.

Education on why America
is hated rather than
letting Americans go on
thinking ~~more~~ they're the
" Greatest ".

MY SUGGESTION:

_____

NEVER DO SOMETHING DRASTIC
JUST FOR THE SAKE OF
A BOY ♥

Beware
of new
enterprises
requiring
new clothes

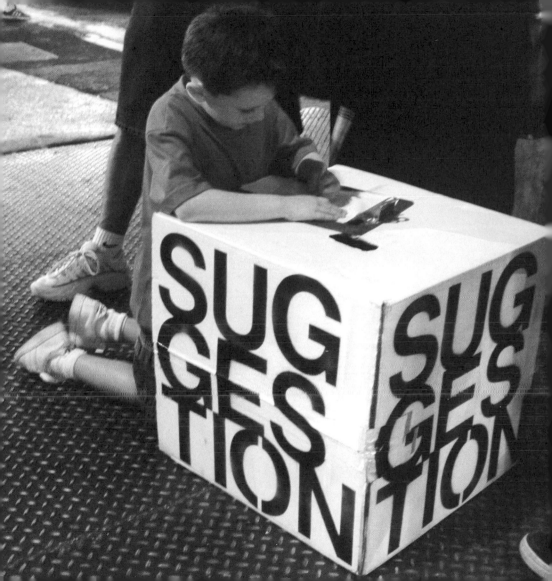

I suggest that everbody relax.

Women shouldn't wear stockings with open toed shoes

build a wall btween
Isarael and palstain
with ((us Army in btween)

People should
use toothpicks
more often.

Women should be more aggresive at picking up on me. ☺
' Cause I'm cute!...'

SMILE
MORE.
SMOKE
LESS.

Homeless people shouldn't yell @ you if you do not donate money to them.

Anger WHAT iS it?
the truth WHAT iS it?
why WAS I LeFt
Alone, And then told
to just understand?
I think the Higer powers
SHould ASK uS For
ForGiveness

THEY SHOULD ANNOUNCE
HOW LONG UNTIL NEXT BUS
OR TRAIN!

PEOPLE Using public
TRANSPORTATION SHould
Always COVER THEiR mouths
WHEN Coughing or SNeezing
IT'S poLiTE. Also, give SeATS
To ELDerly.

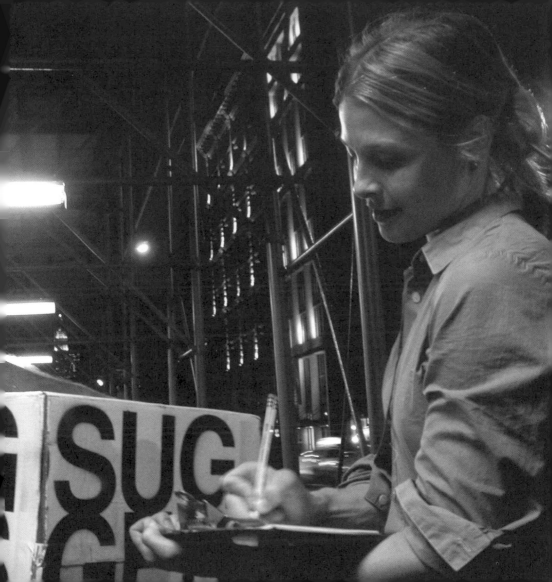

The U.S. needs to take more account of human rights and less of property rights

PEOPLE SHOULD NOT
HANG DOGS THAT LOOK
LIKE THEMSELVES

COPS Will
Let US Skate
bord without getting
Kicked out! or getting
tickets.

We suggest to take down the man.

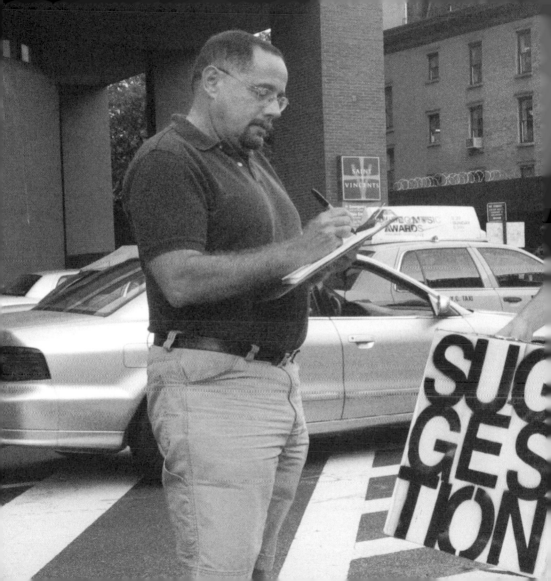

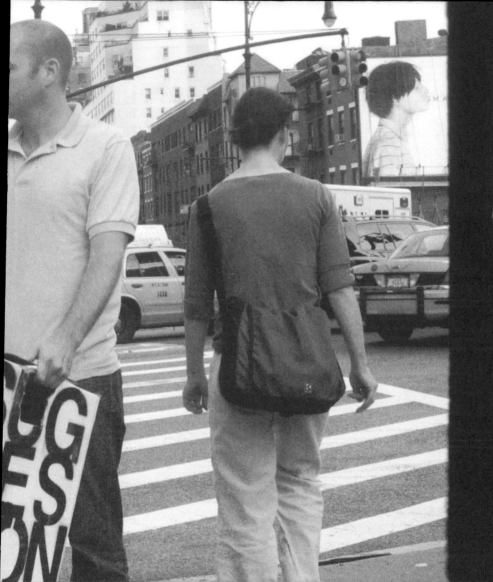

Eat more grey's Papaya!

I suggest that
it be easier
to come out of
the closet.

Say it with a
smile, brother.

And always look

them in the

eye.

XOXO,

8/27/2022

I SUGGEST
THAT MY GIRLFRIEND
BE MORE -
OBJECTIVE !
&
OPEN MINDED !

"God" should give everyone the chance to replay their favorite day before they die

I suggest that we bring back the 10¢ pay phone.

BRING
BACK
THE
PANCHO VILLA
MOUSTACHE —
by any means necessary

Tell that Fucking kid to stop

Kicking my G-d damn seat

Steve

① Get a bigger box

②

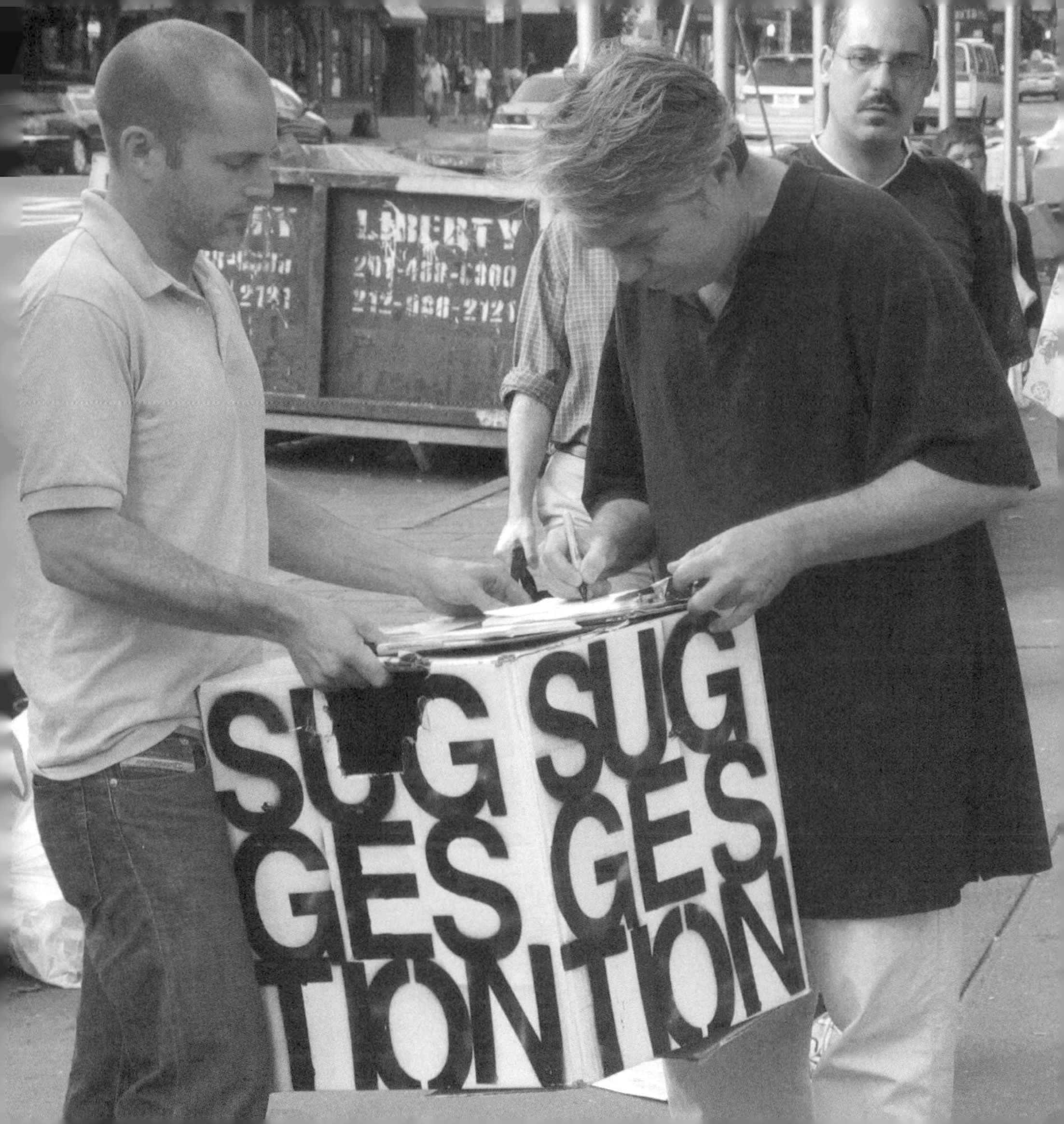
LIBERTY
SUG
GES
TION
SUG
GES
TION

Every body Should
visit Denmark —
Copen hagen

— Great dame —

I would Like to
tell Gov. Pataki
to Kiss my Big
Black Stankin
aSS !!!...

When women get pregnant their husbands/boyfriends have to wear sympathetic fat suits that correspond to the amount of weight the women have gained.

K.D.

I would like a bigger dick

No

More

Meat . . . .

ever

Flush the
huggenheim.
It looks like
a toilet

- Yearround autumn

- non-Pooing puppies

There should be a fine for
trucks ~~of~~ AND suvs parked
at the beginning of a ~~st~~ block,
in front of a stop light.
It is impossible for me to
cross the street with my
baby carriage + see the
oncoming traffic! (and
I'm a jaywalker!)

All I want to say Why many workers annoy of any sight of homtless, Look, Just spare change to them and some day you will have lucky day, if they refuse to spare change to homeless and they are not Kind person as they suppose to love their kids or their wife, tired of hearing from divorce, Domestic Violence!

This person who wrote this Deaf Homeless, was doing Panhandler for 6yrs at 6th Ave/10th St   PEACE

A place
to sit
down .

KILL BARNEY

LETS STOP PRETENDING
THAT WE ARE NEVER
GOING TO DIE.

Don't put
me on the spot

please.

& Lily

I would like to suggest
to the Coca Cola company
to bring back the "New
coke" formula. Classic Coke
is a pathetic attempt at
creating the perfect carbonated
beverage. New coke was
revolutionary.

i suggest

Paper pennies.

Bring back

backrooms.

for sex

in bars.

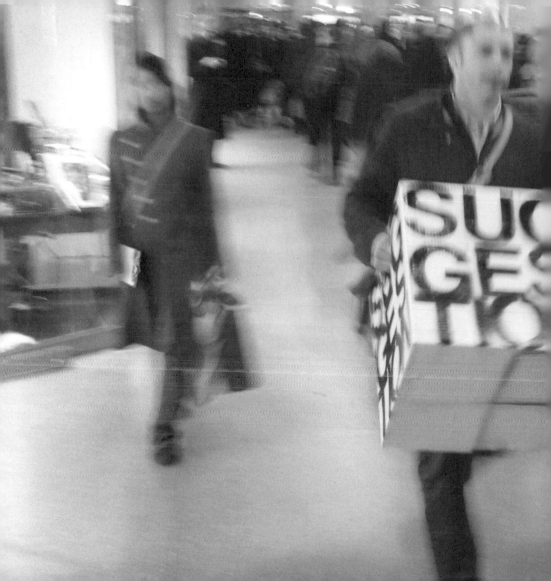

Grand Central Terminal

Next Time Someone
Says Good to See You.

Say Its Good
to be seen

Realize how lucky
you are.

Don't Breathe
under water.

KEEP
CHURCH AND
STATE
SEPERATE

Abolish money

That public schools in NYC
Should have enough money for
2 teachers in every classroom

WASH
YOUR HANDS
BEFORE LEAVING
THE RESTROOM

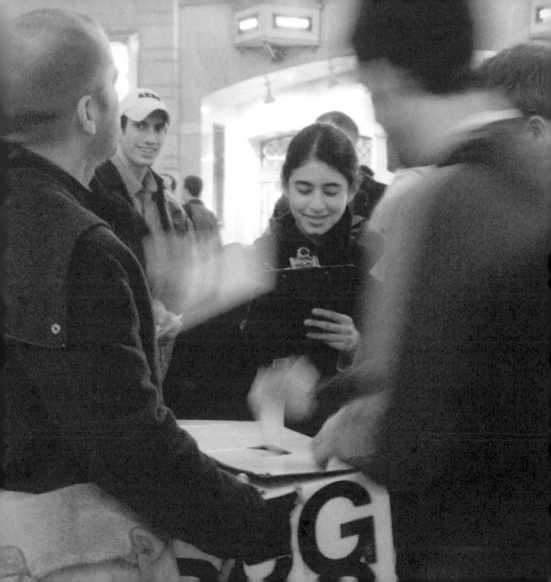

All THESE
Buildings
& Money in
NYC, there
Should be
No one living
On the ~~street~~
St.

go west.

put cheese
inside the
hot dog

put mustard

INSIDE the

pretzel. (like

the cheese hotdog)

VOTE for A

chANgE.

no labels
on fruit

fuck fuck
fuck fuck
fuck.

A girlfriend
who isn't a brain-
less, subservient
cow for my friend
Gustavo

LARRY SHOULD GET A LIFE & QUIT BUGGING ME

I don't have any suggestions.

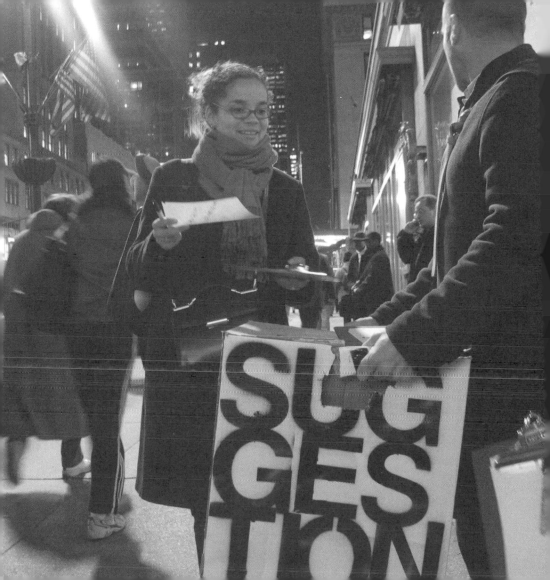

Parents should spend more time w/ their kids & less time worrying abt. what pple think of them

Hair is Hair Women Should Pay the Same amount as Men!

the Lord doesn't want any one to be lost. He wants the best for you. To you want whats best for you. Give your life today to Jesus that wants best for you

STOP Exporting "democracy" and import TRUTH

Find an alternative to gasoline!

EVERYONE TAKE A STEP BACK FROM THEIR CURRENT DESIRES

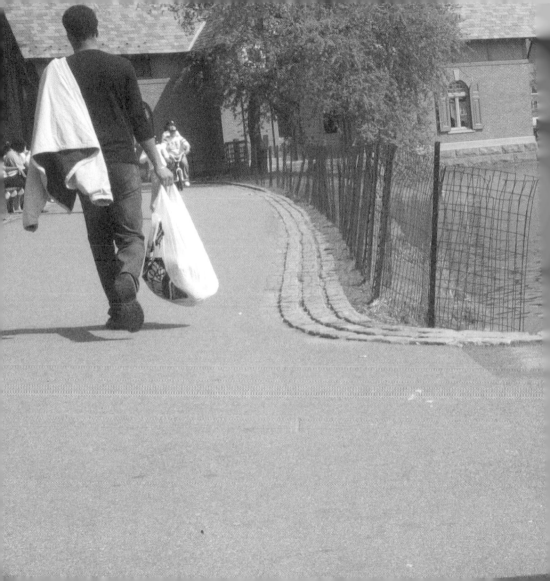

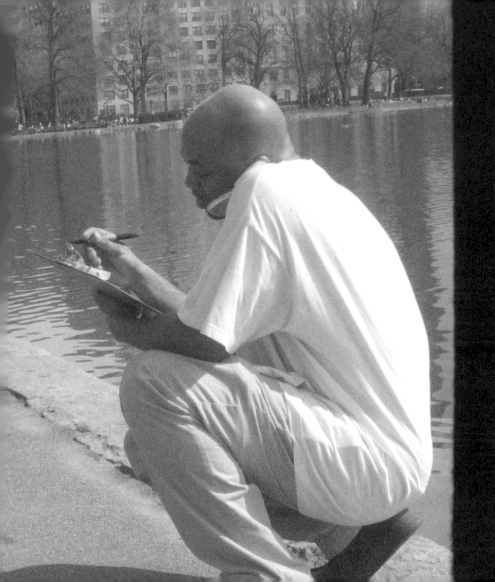

Harlem/Lenox at 110th Street

I serust they put mora Fish in it

RIDEABLE AARDVARKS!

look
beyond
what
you
see.

More
security

WILL THERE EVER
COME A TIME WHEN
MY MISTAKE OF 20 YRS
AGO BE CONSIDERED
INSIGNIFIGANT?
A BROTHER NEEDS A GOOD
JOB

AUSTIN III

S.F.L.
P.B.C.

I WisH I win Lotto so I Can Buy my own PArk

CAPITAL
PUNISHMENT
FOR
PEOPLE
WHO FIND
RELIGION
IN
PRISON

It should be okay to put
a relationship first. ♡

For My Brother to be Quiet

Boys should learn
how to dress better.
Especially my brother.

School is Nice
to Learn From.

legAlize mAriuvgunq

They Should have
~~lockers~~ lockers in
elememtry Schools.

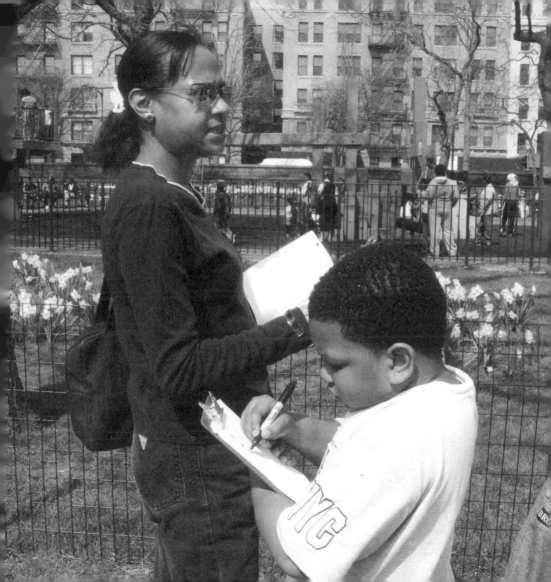

My FirsT Suggestion Is
Put A siGN Stating
AnyOne CauGHT throwing
Rock's In the Water will Be
FineD Pi Geons anD
~~Or~~ ~~Prison~~ DUCKS (Central Parks).

$ TicKeT :

MORE Fellini.
LESS tRophy dogs.

I wish I have a
hamster, a fish Rabbit.
Rabbit.

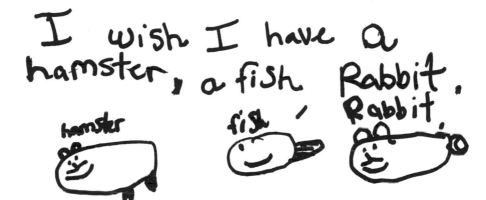

hamster   fish

People should go
after what they
Need not ~~want~~
what they
Want.

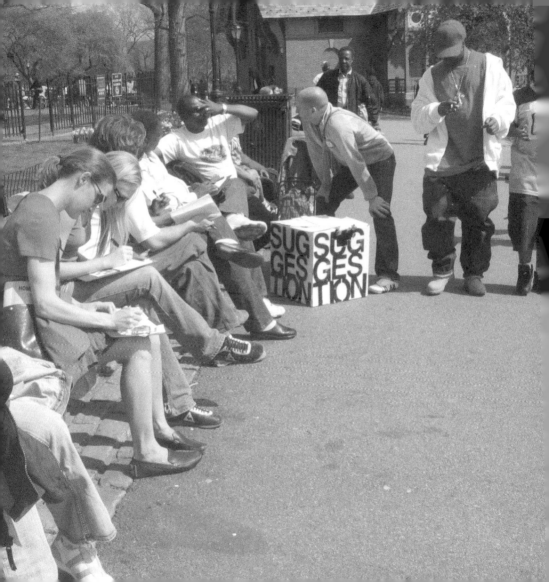

I think that once an individual
goes to prison he/she
should be able to get
employment.
It is called Dept. of
Corrections. Some people
really do change.

I also suggest video
games be less aggressive
and violent.

Single mother · needing financial help from her Children's Father . . . . plus She needs personal Financial help for her Education + her children . . .

I want to be a Successful family man. -Travis

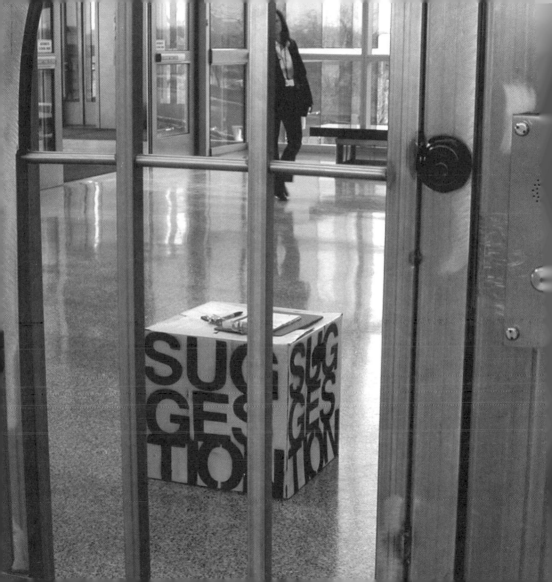

Acknowledgments

First and foremost, we would like to thank the people of New York City and all those who have participated with The Suggestion Box.

We would also like to thank the following for their help, support, and inspiration: Topper Rimel for his participation and contribution to Illegal Art. Thank you. Meghan Ward, Rob Kimball, Piers Roberts, Rory Dodd, Marilyn and Bob Kriegel, Barbara and Bob McDevitt, Natasha Chetiyawardana, Gail and Barry Mallin, Malachi Connolly, Matteo Connolly, Eduardo Rosado, Nashat Akhtar, Jeff Galusha, Marianne McCune, Rob Kimmel, Alonzo Williams, Dorcus Nung, Doug Kriegel, Abby Nocon, Jennifer Nocon, Dave Nyberg, Michael Youmans, Steve Huot, Ashley Rodrigues, Brittany Diaz, Emmit Miller, John Faatz, Tristan Davison, Nicholas Coley, Jason and Kadie Salfi, Annette Brookman, Boozer, Karen Langley, David Horii, George Klauber, Konscious.com, Nylon Technology, WNYC, N.P.R., KVMR, Susan and Neel Doshi, Mark Vegas Abell, Ian Cohen, Kathleen Jayze, Erika Mallin and Barry Latney, Molly Mallin, Joe Salvatore, Bryan Carlin, Designers Block, Ben Galland, Mike Shea, The Cyclone, Gina Alvarez and Stefan Boublil, Martin Ogolter, Gary Friedman and Trish McCall, Kate Spellman, Katinka Matson, Louise Aibel, John Brockman, Sarah Malarkey, Ben Shaykin, Jodi Davis, Victoria Newland, Matt Miller, Oneta and the Silverworks gang, Myrtle Harris, Paul Blake and Ruth Weiss, Barry Negrin, Emmanuel Ronco, Roger K. Sherman, Ron Labuz, Stephen Thomas, Joe Strummer, The Atlantic Ocean, The F-Train, and anyone else who is angry that we forgot to thank you.

Don't ask people to make suggestions while tired

THis is cooL!
You GUYS SHOULD
DO A BOOK.